The DATES &TIMES *of* MESSIAH

JESUS' BIRTHDAY, LENGTH OF MINISTRY, CRUCIFIXION DATE, AND CHRONOLOGY OF GOSPELS PROVEN FROM SCRIPTURE FOR THE FIRST TIME IN TWO THOUSAND YEARS

BRETT HOOPER

This book is adapted from the academic paper *The Dates and Times of Messiah.*
All Bible verses quoted in this book are the author's
translation unless otherwise quoted.

ISBN: 978-0-6450712-5-2 (paperback)
ISBN: 978-0-6450712-6-9 (e-book)
Biblical Fidelity Publishing
Melbourne, Australia
www.biblicalfidelity.com

Contents

Contents

The Dates and Times of Messiah

By Brett D. Hooper MBA, GAICD

1. Abstract

The dating of Jesus' birth, death, and ministry has been studied and debated throughout the last 2,000 years.

Various decent arguments have been made, and enough historical information is available to narrow the timing of these events down to within a small window, but proving the exact dates has seemed beyond the historical information at hand.

The research of Michael Rood, Nehemiah Gordon, and others into the original Hebrew/biblical calendar in recent times has reopened an old and forgotten data set that allows the triangulation of the exact key dates of Jesus when combined with existing historical scholarship in this field.

Sceptics have cast doubt on the reliability of the Gospels as historically accurate accounts of Jesus' life and ministry, doing their best to assign Jesus and the Gospels to the status of mere fable. But fables do not have provable dates; thus, proving the dates goes a long way to proving the historicity of the Gospels and the information they convey. This paper proves, through a combination of scriptural, historical, and astronomical observations verified by internal evidence within the four Gospel accounts, the exact key historical dates of the ministries of Jesus and John the Baptist.

Using the same research methods, this paper also shows that John the Baptist's ministry was three years long and Jesus' ministry was only one year, contradicting 1,700 of church teachings that Jesus' ministry was three years.

The key findings of this paper are:

- Jesus was born on the first day of the Feast of Tabernacles (September 26), 3 BC.
- John's ministry was from Passover AD 27 to Passover AD 30.
- Jesus' ministry proper was one Hebrew year (Passover AD 30 to Passover AD 31).
- Jesus was crucified on April 25, AD 31.
- The verse 6:4 in the Gospel of John is fraudulent.
- With John 6:4 removed, the Gospel of John is chronological.

- The Gospel of Luke is chronological.
- The Gospel of Mark is largely chronological.
- The Gospel of Matthew is *not* chronological.

The practical implications of these findings are significant. With this newly discovered information, it is now possible to render the four Gospels of Jesus into one ordered account, giving clarity and knowability to His life and teachings.

This work of combining the four Gospels into one has been carried out recently by myself in the book *The Gospel of Messiah*, opening the way for others to test this hypothesis more fully and build upon it.

2. Introduction

My aim in writing this paper is to present a logical, reasoned, and evidence-based argument for the dates of Jesus' and John the Baptist's lives and ministries, which are provable.

While it would be ideal to achieve this without appealing to the supernatural, the reader must realise that dealing with God, by definition, means dealing with the supernatural, and it is impossible to prove these dates 2,000 years later purely by a secular/historical method.

The fact that biblical prophecy, parables, general texts, and astronomical observations can be used together to triangulate these important dates is itself a strong proof of the existence of the supernatural. For this reason, this data should also be taken seriously alongside other lines of evidence.

Ruling out the possibility of supernatural explanations holds scientific inquiry hostage to atheism. It ensures the conclusions can have no supernatural element, as these inputs are excluded from the beginning. Genuine scientific inquiry, by definition, must be open to *all* possibilities, and this includes the supernatural.

I've also included a few Bible quotes to educate the non-believing reader on the character of the God of the Bible—and to show the findings are consistent with His proven tendency to leave historical markers for mankind to find as proof of His working throughout history.

I've kept the text that follows as simple as possible in its explanations and arguments, operating on the basis that the simplest explanation of a fact is usually correct (Occam's razor)[1]—and to keep the reader's mind focused on the essential elements of the theory without diverting attention to more detailed and debatable side points. However, as these side points are valuable, I have provided references and appendices for further reading to those interested in digging deeper.

The fact that this theory is simple, with multiple parts that fit together to prove the whole, is its strength. And the whole picture, when seen, provides further proof of the validity and veracity of the individual parts.

Jehovah (God) likes to operate in patterns, but proving this fact is beyond the scope of the following text. The seasoned prophecy student, however, will know this to be true from their experience with the Scriptures and may be an area of future study for those unfamiliar with it.

3. Acknowledgements

The findings of the timing of John's and Jesus' ministries in this paper are original to myself, but I wish to acknowledge the work of Michael Rood and Sir Robert Anderson in this area. While I have differed from their individual findings, I have learned much from them and used components of their theories to construct my own.

Also, the findings in this paper regarding the birthdates of John and Jesus, the visit of the Magi, and the flight and return from Egypt are the work of Michael Rood and not original to me. I have included them in this paper for the sake of having, for the first time, the comprehensive set of dates of Jesus and John in one paper because Jesus' and John's birthdates are important corroborating factors of when their ministries began.

4. The Hebrew Calendar System

In basic terms the ancient Hebrew calendar, as outlined in the Hebrew Bible (Old Testament), is a lunar/agricultural system for calculating months and years.

This calendar follows the cycles of the moon, with the new moon being the sign of a new month. A Hebrew year is generally twelve months (cycles of the moon) and is calibrated to the sun periodically through the barley harvest in Israel, requiring a thirteenth month to be added at times (approximately every 2.7 years on average).

This calendar system ensures the start of the barley harvest is always in the first month of the Hebrew year, which is required to fulfil the requirements of the Feast of Firstfruits set out by Moses in the Torah (Leviticus 23:9–14).

It may also be helpful to the reader to understand the timing of the major Feasts of Israel relative to the Western calendar system before reading further.

Spring Feasts[2]

- Passover, Unleavened Bread, and Firstfruits—1st Hebrew month (~APR)
- Weeks (a.k.a. Pentecost) —3rd Hebrew month (~JUN)

Autumn Feasts[1]

- Day of Trumpets—7th Hebrew month (~SEP)
- Day of Atonement—7th Hebrew month (~SEP/OCT)
- Tabernacles—7th Hebrew month (~SEP/OCT)

Winter Feast[1]

- Feast of Lights (a.k.a. Hanukkah)—9th Hebrew month (~DEC)

The main point the reader needs to understand before proceeding is that the God of the Hebrew Bible claims (through Moses) that He put the sun, moon, and stars in the sky for signs and His appointed times (Genesis 1:14).

Unfortunately the Hebrew word for appointed times (*moedim*) has been translated in English Bibles as *seasons* for hundreds of years. This gives a false impression of the text.

Moedim (plural of *moed*) is an important concept in Scripture as it relates not only to the heavenly bodies but also to the tabernacle Moses set up (tent of the *moed*; Exodus 27:21) and the Feasts of Jehovah (the *moed* of Jehovah; Leviticus 23:2). All three are referred to as the *moedim* (appointed times) of Jehovah and point forward to the fulfilment of the appointed times of God.

The non-believing reader may wonder why telling the future has a place in an academic paper. In some way approximately 56%[3] of the world's population believes in the God of the Bible and has done so (in larger percentages) for 2,000 years—and the Jews for 2,000 years prior to that. One of this deity's claims to being the Creator is that He can tell what will take place in the future (Amos 3:7; Isaiah 46:10), and that is the essence of this paper—I have found proof of that by proving the dates of God's anointed (Messiah, or Christ) using Scripture and astronomical observations. If the reader does not believe in this deity, that's their personal choice, but with 56% of the world believing in

Him, and the recorded history of the world largely involving Him, understanding Him, in large part, is understanding history itself and the world we live in.

5. Births of John the Baptist and Jesus

To derive the birthdates and ministries of John the Baptist and Jesus, it is important to treat these cousins as a pair, as their lives are intertwined, and one data set allows the computation of the other.

Unlike the dates of their ministries and Jesus' death, the calculations of their birthdays are not original to this paper. Michael Rood and others found these dates earlier using the same basic method I have used in finding the ministry and crucifixion dates.

An explanation of these dates is included here, as establishing these dates as *factual* is important to proving the dates original to this paper, as it is clear from the Gospel of Luke (3:23) that Jesus was about thirty years old when He began His ministry.

5.1. The Birth of Jesus

There is an important principle in Scripture that God does nothing without first revealing it to His servants the prophets (Amos 3:7). This allows the people of God to know if an event is from God or not, as only He can tell the end from the beginning (Isaiah 46:10).

This principle is exhibited in the Feasts of Jehovah found in Leviticus 23. There were three major Feasts of Israel given through Moses to the children of Israel in the sixteenth century BC. They are:

- Unleavened Bread (including Passover and Firstfruits)
- Weeks (a.k.a. Pentecost)
- Tabernacles

The Feast of Passover is known to be prophetic of Jesus' death and Pentecost of the giving of the Holy Spirit to Jesus' disciples. But the Feast of Tabernacles is also about Jesus' life and points to His birthday!

In Psalm 40:7, it is written:

> Then said I, Lo, I come: in the volume of the book it is written of Me.

Most take this to be speaking of Messiah, and many Christians believe the bulk of the Old Testament is written of the (then) coming Messiah. If this is true, it makes sense that the Feast of Tabernacles is about the Messiah's life too.

Several Old Testament concepts are prophetic pictures that point to the reality of Jesus the Messiah and His birth into this world.

5.1.1. The Tabernacle as the Body of Christ

A typology runs through the Bible relating to the house of God. Different words are used for it (tabernacle [tent], temple, house), but they're all pointing to the one central building where Jehovah said He would put His Name (Deuteronomy 12; 1 Kings 8). God says to King David in 2 Samuel 7:11–14:

> Also Jehovah tells you that He will make you a house. And when your days are fulfilled, and you shall sleep with your fathers, I will set up your seed (descendant) after you, which shall proceed out of your bowels, and I will establish his kingdom. He shall build a house for My Name, and I will establish the throne of his kingdom forever. I will be his father, and he shall be My son.

Two notable places in the New Testament that mention the tabernacle/temple of God are in John 1:14 and 2:19, which read respectively:

> And the Word became flesh, and dwelt (tabernacled) among us, and we saw His glory, the glory of the only begotten of the Father, full of grace and truth.

> Jesus answered and said to them, "Tear down this temple, and in three days I will raise it up." Then said the Jews, "Forty-six years was this temple in building,[4] and will You raise it up again in three days?" But He spoke of the temple of His body.

These verses speak of Jesus' advent to Earth, when the second member of the Trinity was made flesh and dwelt among us. Thus, these references allude to His incarnation and birth, and because John refers to Jesus' body twice as the tabernacle/temple of God, this is a strong clue that the Feast of Tabernacles was prophetic of Jesus' birth.

Leviticus 23:33–36 reveals the first day of the Feast was a high holy day, and the eight day was a high holy day. It can be supposed from this that the first day of the Feast of Tabernacles signifies Jesus' birthday and the eighth day His circumcision (Luke 2:21). Again, a pattern is evident, and Jesus—being born on the first day of the Feast and then circumcised on the eighth day—fits the pattern laid down by Moses 1,500 years earlier.

5.1.2. The Feast of Lights

The Feast of Lights (Hanukkah) is another event that points to Jesus and helps calculate His birth date.

The Jews instituted this Feast to commemorate the anniversary of the rededication of the temple in Jerusalem (164 BC) after the Greeks had desecrated it during a period when they tried to assimilate the Jews into their pagan culture and religious practice.

It is called the Feast of Lights because it is said the Jews had only enough oil to keep the menorah burning in the temple for one day during the rededication, but the menorah miraculously burnt for eight days until new oil could be sourced.

Interestingly, the distance between the Feast of Lights and the Feast of Tabernacles when Jesus was born is the length of a woman's gestation period. Given the typology around Jesus as the light of the world (John 1:4–5 and 8:12), it can be supposed that the Feast of Lights is when Jesus was conceived by the Holy Spirit.

5.1.3. Homage to the King

When a theory is correctly interpreted, you will often find seemingly obscure peripheral evidence for it.

One such piece of evidence supporting Jesus' birth on Tabernacles is found in Zechariah 14:16–17, which speaks of a yet-future time where God's anointed King is to be worshipped in Jerusalem:

> And it shall come to pass, that everyone that is left of all the nations who came against Jerusalem shall go up from year to year to worship the King, Jehovah of hosts, and keep the Feast of Tabernacles.
>
> And it shall be, that whosoever will not come up, of all the families of the earth, to Jerusalem to worship the King, Jehovah of hosts, even upon them shall be no rain.

A study of the term "Jehovah of Hosts" in the Old Testament reveals this person is in fact the second member of the Trinity (the Son), and indeed the name Jesus (Yeshua in Hebrew) literally means "Jehovah-saves." Therefore, it is not a strange thing to call Jesus "Jehovah," showing Jesus as the King to be worshipped in Jerusalem.

What better time to pay homage to the King than on His birthday! This is a subjective point on its own but supports other stronger evidence that Tabernacles is Jesus' birthday.

5.1.4. Revelation 12:1

The key factor in selecting 3 BC as the year of Jesus' birth is that the star sign of His birth occurs this year as per Revelation 12:1, which reads:

> And there appeared a great sign in heaven; a woman clothed with the sun, and the moon under her feet, and upon her head a crown of twelve stars: and she being with child cried, travailing in birth, and pained to be delivered.

And Revelation 12:5, reads:

> And she brought forth a male Child, who was to rule all nations with a rod of iron: and her Child was caught up to God, and to His throne.

That these passages signify the birth of Messiah is supported in Isaiah 7, where King Ahaz (eighth century BC) is told to ask for a sign from Jehovah in either the depths below or the heavens above. Ahaz refuses to ask, so Isaiah tells him what the sign will be (v. 14):

> Behold, the virgin shall conceive and bear a Son, and shall call His name Immanuel (God among us).

OPPOSITE PAGE: A representation of the woman (a.k.a. Virgo, the virgin) clothed with the sun, the new moon at her feet (first day of the seventh Hebrew month), and a crown of twelve stars upon her head (nine stars in Leo plus Mercury, Venus, and Jupiter).[5]

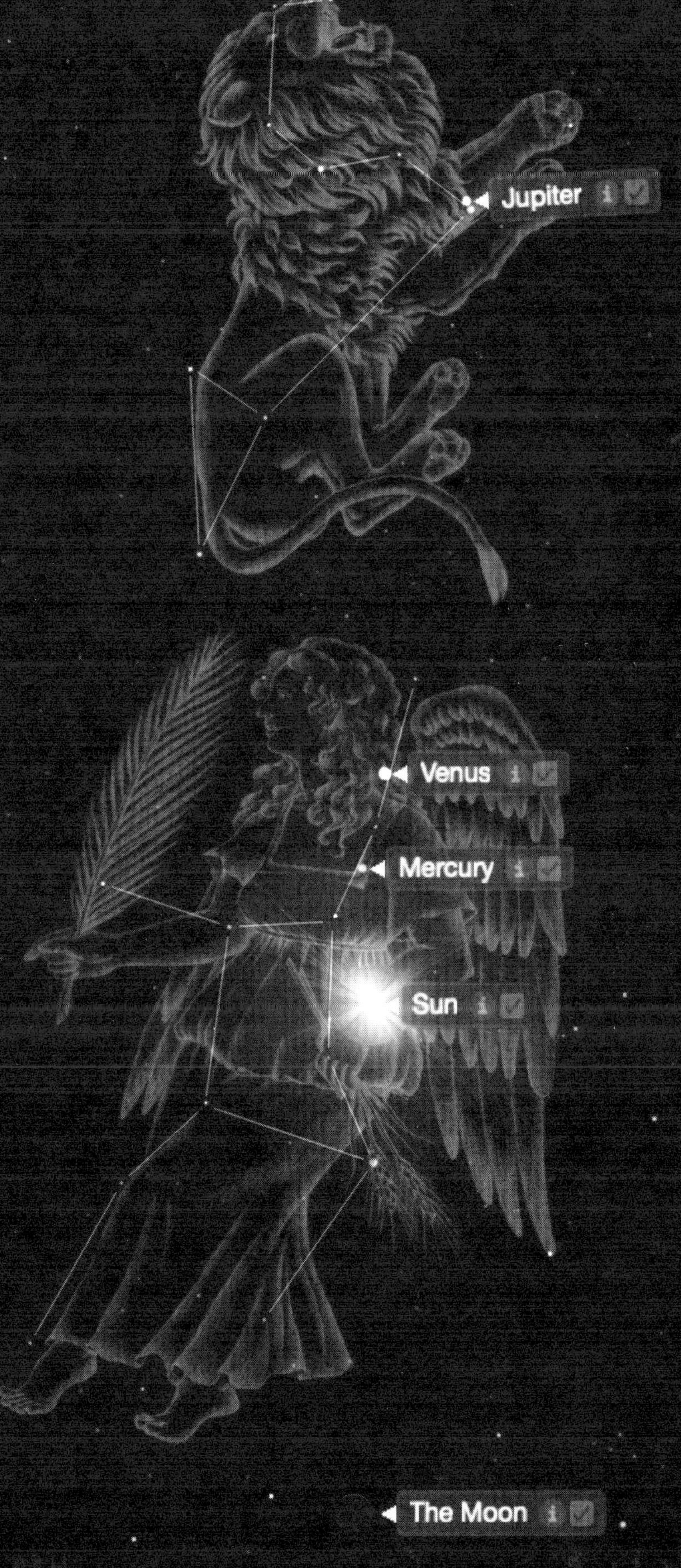
Jupiter
Venus
Mercury
Sun
The Moon

The woman, then, is clearly the Virgin Mary and the Son clearly Jesus, as this reflects perfectly Luke 1:30–35:

> And the angel said to her, "Fear not Mary, for you have found grace with God. And behold, you shall conceive in your womb and bring forth a Son, and shall call His Name Jesus. He shall be great and shall be called the Son of the Most High; and the Lord Jehovah shall give to Him the throne of His father David. He shall reign over the house of Jacob forever, and of His kingdom there shall be no end."
>
> Then said Mary to the angel, "How shall this be, seeing I have not known a man?" And the angel answered and said to her, "The Holy Spirit shall come to you, and the power of the Most High shall overshadow you; therefore the Holy One who shall be born of you shall be called the Son of God!"

This astronomical sign appeared on September 12 (Day of Trumpets), 3 BC. I suppose from this (as does Michael Rood) that this day heralds the birth of Messiah two weeks later, the first day of the Feast of Tabernacles (September 26).

5.2. The Birth of John the Baptist

Knowing these details it is merely a matter of deducing John the Baptist's birthday by subtracting six Hebrew months from Jesus' birthday (Luke 1:36).

When done, it is noticed that the Passover is six months before the Feast of Tabernacles when Jesus was born. As God likes to do things in patterns, assume that John was born on the day of Passover 3 BC.[6]

Interestingly there is an extrabiblical tradition that provides evidence of the timing of John's birthday.

Jewish families to this day leave an extra chair at the table at the Passover meal as they expect Elijah the prophet to return on Passover. Taking this alongside Jesus' comment that John was the Elijah to come (Matthew 11:14) confirms John's birthday and the fact that his ministry likely began on Passover being his birthday.

Luke provides further evidence for the approximate timing of John's and Jesus' birthdays when he says that John's father, Zechariah, was in the priestly course of Abijah.

According to 1 Chronicles 24, the descendants of Abijah were to serve as the eighth course of priests in the temple service. According to Rood each course served twice in the year for a week at a time during the normal course of the year, with multiple courses serving during the major Feasts, such as Passover.[7]

This puts the time of Zechariah's first of two periodic services in the temple for the year at or around Pentecost when the angel appeared to Him. This is just the right amount of time (gestation period) for Zechariah to go home and for John to be conceived and born on Passover.

This is speculative on its own, but when combined with the evidence of Jesus' birth on Tabernacles, helps confirm the timing of John's birth.

5.3. Birth of Jesus Consistent with Herod's Death

Josephus gives an account of the timing of Herod's death, and that the following event happens not long before Herod's death (*Antiquities of the Jews, Book XVII,* Para. 167):

> Herod deprived this Matthias of the high priesthood, and burnt alive the other Matthias, who had raised the sedition, with his other accomplices. And that very night there was an eclipse of the moon.

Because of this quoted eclipse of the moon in Josephus, most scholars date Herod's death just after the eclipse of March 12, 4 BC. The problem is that Jesus had to be born before Herod died, as this was the Herod who tried to kill Jesus as an infant (Matthew 2:16)—therefore, many scholars put Jesus' birth around 6 BC.

There is however an even more impressive lunar eclipse on January 9–10, 1 BC. This also fits Josephus' account, aligns better with the heavenly sign in Revelation 12:1 (September 3 BC), and corresponds with the baptism of Jesus occurring at about thirty years of age.

5.4. Consistent with Jesus' Ministry Start Date

As per Luke 3:23, Jesus was about thirty years old when He was baptised and began His ministry. When Jesus' birthday from this part of the paper is combined with the later finding that Jesus was baptised on February 12, AD 30, it is seen that Jesus was thirty-one-years-and-four-months old at this time (about thirty).

6. Visit of the Magi in 2 BC

Consistent with the finding that Jesus and John were born in 3 BC are the star signs the Magi followed to find the infant King.

The star sign in Revelation 12:1 has already been reviewed, being the major sign, but there were a series of astronomical conjunctions of Jupiter with other heavenly bodies, which seem to have been the guiding star that led the Magi to Bethlehem.

According to Rood[8] these conjunctions and dates are:

- Jupiter/Venus, August 1, 3 BC
- Jupiter/Regulus, September 12, 3 BC (part of Revelation 12:1)
- Jupiter/Regulus, February 17, 2 BC
- Jupiter/Regulus, May 8, 2 BC
- Jupiter/Venus, June 17, 2 BC
- Jupiter/Mercury/Venus/Mars, August 27, 2 BC
- Jupiter/Venus, October 13, 2 BC
- Jupiter in retrograde (appearing to stand still over Bethlehem), December 21, 2 BC

It should be noted that the Jewish prophet Daniel was the head of the Magi six centuries earlier, he being the link between the Magi and the Jewish Messiah and likely the reason the Magi had knowledge to look out for and follow these signs in the heavens.

Given the timing of these conjunctions, the Magi would have visited Jesus when He was fifteen months old. This is consistent with Herod killing all the infants around Bethlehem under two years of age. If Jesus was a newborn at the time of the visit of the Magi, killing up to two years of age seems excessive. Killing infants six months to one year of age would have been plenty of safety margin for Herod to ensure he removed his new rival.

The Magi's gift of gold to Jesus' family is significant because at forty days old, Jesus' parents only offered the poor-man's sacrifice to God (Luke 2:24; Leviticus 12:1–8), showing they did not yet have the gold. It can be deduced that the gift of gold was given to the family after the forty days and not at the time of Jesus' birth as told in popular culture.

7. Flight to Egypt

It is likely the gold from the Magi was God's provision for the family to live in exile in Egypt after Herod's attempt on Jesus' life.

According to Rood, Jesus' family fled to Egypt in late December 2 BC at the time of the murder of the innocents. Rood also speculates that the family returned to Israel during the spring of 1 BC directly after Herod the Great's death.[9]

8. John's Ministry Dates

The first key finding original to this paper is the dating and length of John the Baptist's ministry. I have calculated this data by triangulating three points of Scripture, which I'll now review individually.

8.1. Fifteenth Year of Tiberius Caesar

The historian and Gospel writer Dr. Luke provides the starting date of John the Baptist's ministry in Roman terms (Luke 3:1–2):

> Now in the fifteenth year of the reign of Tiberius Caesar, Pontius Pilate being governor of Judea … the word of God came to John the son of Zechariah in the wilderness.

The problem with converting this information into the Julian calendar is in how reginal years are counted and deciding which is the correct start year for Tiberius.

Most secular historians tell us that Tiberius began to co-reign with his stepfather in AD 12 and exclusively in AD 14 with Augustus' death. Which year the start of Tiberius' reign should be counted from is argued by those trying to calculate this date.

Historians also argue over whether a reginal year begins from the date an emperor starts his reign or whether the remainder of that year is credited to the old monarch and the new monarch's reign nominally starts from the next calendar year.

With this uncertainty in the method of reginal calculation, the potential start years of John's ministry range from AD 27 to AD 30.

There is a speculative way to narrow these dates down further, however.

Many expositors in the past have focused on the fact that Jesus was a high priest in the order of Melchizedek (Psalm 110:4; Hebrews 7:17) and speculated that Jesus entered His ministry at age thirty. However, I believe this is a category error, as nothing is spoken of in the Bible regarding age for that priesthood.

John the Baptist, however, was eligible to be a priest in the order of Aaron, and male descendants of Aaron entered that priesthood at thirty (Numbers 4:3). This is the dating method that should have been looked at all along.

There is a problem here too. Does John become eligible for the priesthood in his thirtieth year (his twenty-ninth birthday) or on his thirtieth birthday? Assuming John turned his back on the priesthood and began his ministry on the day he was eligible to become a priest (God loves patterns), this narrows the starting day down to John's birthday on Passover AD 27 or Passover AD 28. This gives credence to the fact that the calculation should start from AD 12 when Tiberius began to co-reign as emperor with his stepfather.

This is speculative to be sure, but this speculation fits cohesively into a larger cumulative picture that will come together throughout this paper.

8.2. Parable of the Barren Fig Tree

There are a distinct lack of theories on the length of John's ministry. The Gospel of Luke tells us how long it is, however, and it seems no one in the last 2,000 years has understood it. In Luke 13:6–9, Jesus, in His parable of the barren fig tree, states:

> A certain man had a fig tree planted in his vineyard, and he came and sought fruit thereon, and found none. Then he said to the keeper of his vineyard, "Behold, these three years I came seeking fruit upon this fig tree, and found none! Cut it down, why does it encumber the ground?" And he answering, said to him, "Lord, leave it alone this year also, till I shall dig about it and throw manure upon it. If it bears fruit, good; and if not, then after that you shall cut it down!"

Notice that this parable doesn't say "all these years"; it has a defined period of time, "these three years." This gives us the time of John the Baptist's ministry, the three years of the fig tree (Israel) not bearing fruit (corporately) under his ministry of repentance.

The one more year requested by the keeper of the vineyard (Jesus) on behalf of the fig tree represents His ministry proper, which is one Hebrew year, as shall be proven later in this paper.

If my interpretation of the parable of the barren fig tree is correct, the length of John's ministry and the length of Jesus' ministry is now known; and when the end of Jesus' ministry is calculated by other means, the correct candidate year for the start of John's ministry will be verified.

8.3. The End of John's Ministry

John's ministry physically ends when he is either thrown in prison or executed by Herod.

Given the parable of the barren fig tree, however, I suspect in God's eyes, there is a nominal end to John's ministry and start of Jesus'. I say nominal because it is clear from the Gospels that both John and Jesus ministered at the same time for a period of a few months.

Given that all Jesus did at the start of His ministry was undergo forty days of testing in the wilderness and call His first disciples (no miracles were recorded during this period except the wedding feast at Cana, which was a private miracle for His disciples), I suggest that this period up until the final Passover of John's ministry (which was also the first Passover of Jesus' ministry), was nominally John's and part of his three years, as per the parable of the barren fig tree.

Thus, when the date of the crucifixion is reviewed in the next section, it is possible to calculate back to the nominal end of John's ministry.

9. Jesus' Crucifixion Year

This is the category of evidence that has the strongest proof and can be used to calculate and verify other related dates. As such, I will prove the year of the crucifixion before I look at the length of Jesus' ministry.

9.1. Day of the Week

Jesus said He would be three days and three nights in the grave (Matthew 12:40). Combining this with the understanding that Jesus was killed on Passover is a great help in determining the crucifixion year.
Passover can fall on any day of the week as it always takes place on the fourteenth of Nisan (the night that follows the killing of the Passover is generally the full moon of the first Hebrew month). It is not fixed to a certain day of the week.

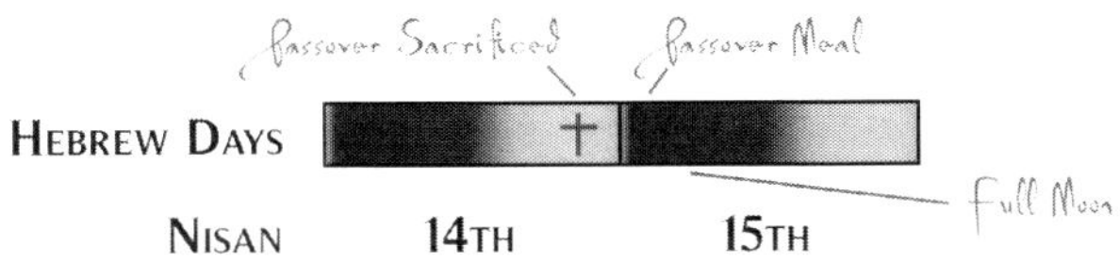

The resurrection (Firstfruits), however, will always be on the first day of the Hebrew week (Leviticus 23:10–11) and is reported as being so in the Gospels. This means the number of days between Passover and Firstfruits changes from year to year.

It is known that Jesus rose on the first day of the Hebrew week (Saturday sunset to Sunday sunset in the Western system). Counting back three days and three nights (Matthew 12:39–40) means that Jesus must have been crucified on a Wednesday afternoon.

This day of the week is also verified by the text of the Gospels themselves when Mark's and Luke's account are taken together; this is seen by solving a riddle:

> How is it possible that the women prepared the spices for Jesus' burial and then rested on the sabbath (Luke 23:56), and then, when the sabbath had passed, the women bought (purchased) the spices (Mark 16:1)?

Both things cannot be true unless:

- There's a contradiction between Mark and Luke; or,
- There are two sabbaths in view.

Unfortunately many people jump on the first option seeing an opportunity to discredit the Gospels as historically accurate. The second option however is correct—no contradiction—and it gives a second witness to the three days and three nights Jesus foretold before His death. It should be noted, Matthew 28:1 says in Greek, *after the Sabbaths* (plural), giving further evidence that the Sabbath in Luke 23:56 and Sabbath in Mark 16:1 were different Sabbaths.

When read together, the Gospels show the following timeline:

Nisan 14 (Wednesday Afternoon)
- The women watched where Jesus was laid to rest (Matthew 27:61; Luke 23:55).

Nisan 15 (Wednesday Sunset to Thursday Sunset)
- They rested on the sabbath (inferred) being the first day of the Feast of Unleavened Bread (Leviticus 23:7).

Nisan 16 (Thursday Sunset to Friday Sunset)
- They purchased and prepared the burial spices (Mark 16:1; Luke 23:56).

Nisan 17 (Friday Sunset to Saturday Sunset)

- They rested on the weekly sabbath as per the commandment (Luke 23:56).

Nisan 18 (Saturday Sunset to Sunday Sunset)

- The women came to the tomb with the spices early the first day of the week (Matthew 28:1; Mark 16:2; Luke 24:1; John 20:1).

Understanding that the Passover moon (full moon) needed to take place the night of the Passover (Nisan 15), as per the Hebrew calendar system, and that the Passover took place on a Wednesday afternoon allows us, through astronomical observation, to calculate back into history and see that only AD 28 and AD 31 fit this criterion.[10]

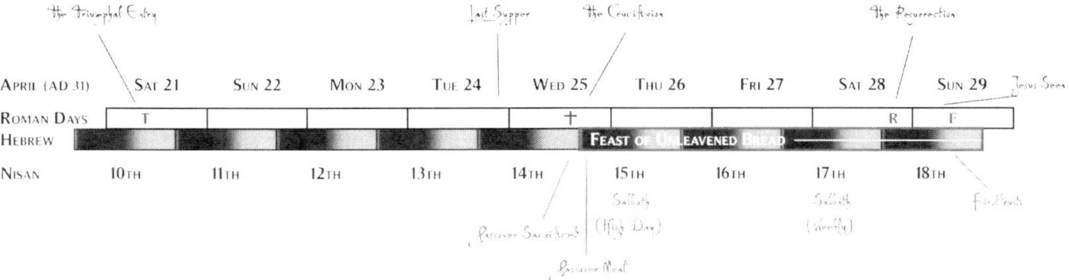

**Please see the appendices for more information on the day of the week the crucifixion took place and more textual evidence for it.*

9.2. Blood Moon

In the book of Acts, Peter provides another strong historical marker that can be used to deduce the year of the crucifixion. Quoting the prophet Joel, he says on the day of Pentecost that year (Acts 2:19–20):

> I (Jehovah) will show wonders in heaven above and signs in the earth beneath: blood and fire and billows of smoke. The sun shall be turned into darkness, and <u>the moon into blood</u>.

It's clear from this statement that the year of the crucifixion must have a blood moon. Using the data set from NASA's *Five Millennium of Lunar Eclipses*, it is seen that only AD 31, AD 32, and AD 33 have blood moons in the candidate set; however, AD 32 was not visible from Israel, so that year must be ruled out.

On April 3, AD 33, the moon arose in the last stage of a partial eclipse, but according to Schaefer in his peer-reviewed paper *Lunar Visibility and the Crucifixion,* p. 65:

This is like trying to spot an 8-watt red light bulb next to a megawatt search-light.

This blood moon was barely visible to the people in Jerusalem and is not a good candidate for the blood moon Peter was referring to on the day of Pentecost.

This leaves us with only one candidate year, AD 31. This observation, combined with a Wednesday Passover, proves that AD 31 is the only candidate year the crucifixion could have taken place.

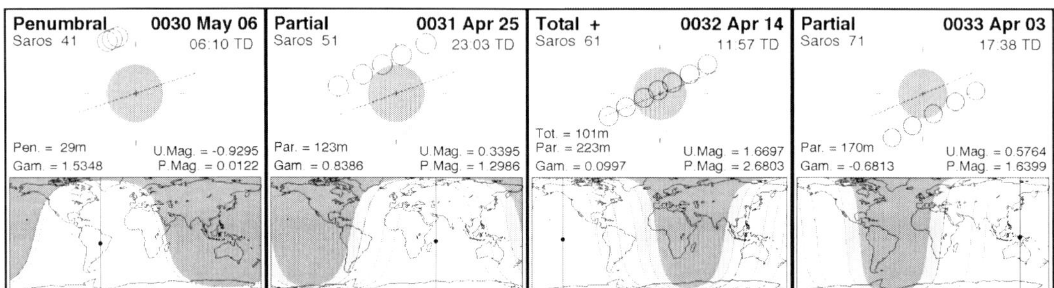

ABOVE: Candidate eclipses around the time of Passover AD 27–34. The white zones on the images denote where the eclipse was visible from.[11]

9.3. Thirteen-Month Year

In the text of the Gospels, there is an interesting occurrence where Jesus does a loop from Jerusalem, up through Samaria, into the Galilee, back down through Perea, and then into Jerusalem for His final Passover (John 11:54; Luke 17:11–19; Matthew 20:17; Mark 10:1, 32; Luke 18:31–33).

It seems as if Jesus was ready for the Passover near Jerusalem and then had a spare month to fill in before going back for the Passover a month later. This is exactly what would be expected in a Hebrew leap year.

Under the biblical Hebrew calendar, when the barley isn't ripe for the Feast of Unleavened Bread (this Feast is based around the barley harvest), an additional thirteenth month is added to the year, which fulfils the requirement of the Feast and keeps the Hebrew lunar system in synchronisation with the sun over time.

Only AD 31 is definitively a thirteen-month year in this period with AD 28, 29, and 34 being potentially so. As will be shown later, thirteen months in the year of Jesus' ministry is required to fulfil the seventy-week prophecy of Daniel.

9.4. Daniel's Sixty-Nine-Week Prophecy

There is a clear prophecy in the book of Daniel (sixth century BC) telling the exact time Messiah would come and be cut off (killed). It is known as the seventy-week prophecy of Daniel (Daniel 9:24–26):

> Seventy weeks (sevens) are determined upon your people and upon your holy city, to finish the transgression, and to make an end of sins, and to make reconciliation for iniquity, and to bring in everlasting righteousness, and to seal up the vision and prophecy, and to anoint the most holy.
>
> Know therefore and understand—from the going forth of the commandment to restore and to build Jerusalem until Messiah the prince shall be seven weeks, and sixty-two weeks. The street shall be built again, and the wall, even in troublesome times.
>
> And after sixty-two weeks Messiah shall be cut-off, but not for Himself.

I have titled this section the Sixty-Nine-Week Prophecy rather than the seventy weeks mentioned in the text because there are two prophecies here that have been confused as one: a seventy-week prophecy and a sixty-nine-week prophecy. The sixty-nine-week prophecy will be dealt with here and the seventy-week prophecy later in the paper.

Sixty-nine weeks are derived by adding the seven-weeks of the prophecy to the sixty-two weeks. The time periods here are assumed by most to be years, so the prophecy is generally taken as 483 years (69 x 7 years).

Most expositors generally pick their favoured crucifixion year, subtract 483 years, and speculate that computed year as the start date of the decree to restore and rebuild Jerusalem. The problem with this approach is that the Bible gives the exact starting date, and that must be followed. It is found in the book of Nehemiah 2:1–5:

> It came to pass in the month Nisan, in the twentieth year of Artaxerxes the king, that wine was before him: and I took up the wine and gave it unto the king. Now I had not been sad in his presence before. Therefore, the king said to me, "Why is your countenance sad, seeing you are not sick? This is nothing more than sorrow of heart."
>
> Then I was very afraid, and said to the king, "Let the king live forever: why should not my countenance be sad, when the city, the place of my fathers'

> tombs, lay in ruins, and the gates of it burnt with fire?" Then the king said to me, "What is your request?" So I prayed to the God of heaven. And I said to the king, "If it please the king, and if your servant has found favour in your sight, send me to Judah, to the city of my fathers' tombs, that I may build it."

Here it is clearly stated that the decree to rebuild Jerusalem was given in the twentieth year of Artaxerxes. Secular scholars date the start of Artaxerxes reign to August 465 BC.[12]

Again, the problem of how to reckon reginal years arises, so a date range of 446–445 BC will be allowed to cover all possibilities for the twentieth year of Artaxerxes.

If 483 solar years are added to the proposed start dates, the result comes out at AD 38–39, which is outside the generally accepted range of candidate years as the result does not fit other historical information regarding the life of Jesus; this is why others vary the start date. However, it turns out they should have been looking more closely at how the time interval is calculated and not trying to massage the start date.

There is nothing to say the 483 time periods are solar years, and it was Sir Robert Anderson (a nineteenth-century Scotland Yard detective) who realized these time periods were a nominal 360 days.

Anderson noted that in Revelation 11–13, a nominal month was thirty days and a nominal year (a time) was twelve months. He called this time period of 360 days a prophetic year and noted that Julius Africanus (a Christian historian) also held this view in the third century.[13]

Anderson calculated that the twentieth year of Artaxerxes was 445 BC and counted forward 173,880 days (69 x 7 x 360) and came out in April AD 32.

I have adopted Anderson's prophetic-year theory as it is scripturally consistent and respects the known starting point of Daniel's prophecy as recorded in Nehemiah. However, Anderson has miscalculated the start year; I have it at 446 BC, and this is where we differ.

To keep things simple, I'm going to allow all possible dates (446–445 BC) and their outcomes of AD 31–32 and prove the date of the crucifixion by verification with other data points.

10. Summary So Far

AD 31 is the only year that meets every criterion without fail, confirming this was the year Jesus died. Additional proof, supplied following, strengthens the claim that the barren fig tree parable is reliable for calculating the dates of John's and Jesus' ministries.

The table below reviews the arguments for an AD 31 crucifixion:

	AD 27	AD 28	AD 29	AD 30	AD 31	AD 32	AD 33	AD 34
30th of John & 3+1					Y	Y		
Day of Week		Y			Y			Y
Blood Moon					Y		Y	
13th Month		Y	Y		Y			Y
69-Weeks Prophecy					Y	Y		
Strength of Argument		**40%**	**20%**		**100%**	**40%**	**20%**	**20%***

* *The year AD 34 may have either a Wednesday Passover or thirteen-month year but cannot have both. Hence, I have only counted one of the Yeses in the Strength of Argument calculation.*

11. Jesus' Ministry Dates

Additional proof for AD 31 as the year of Jesus' crucifixion includes both scriptural and extrabiblical evidence.

The Gospels of Matthew, Mark, and Luke read as if Jesus' ministry is one year long. This is admitted by Eusebius of Caesarea, the leading proponent of the three-and-a-half-year ministry theory (hereafter called the three-year ministry). In his book *Church History, Book III,* Ch. XXIV, he states:

> It is evident that the three evangelists [Matthew, Mark, and Luke] record only the deeds done by the Saviour for only one year after the imprisonment of John the Baptist and indicated this in the beginning of their account.

The Gospel of John also reads as if it's only one year long—except for John 6:4, which adds another Passover into the timeline and makes Jesus' ministry at least two years.

A large part of the remainder of this paper will prove that John 6:4 was a late addition to the Gospel of John and should not be in the text. First, however, consider why Scripture does not support a three-year ministry.

11.1. The Three-Year Ministry

Most Christians today accept Jesus' ministry as having been three years long, as that is what they have been taught. This has been church doctrine for 1,700 years, meaning it is assumed into nearly every Bible commentary and doctrinal article written since the fourth century.

Tradition is powerful—and 1,700 years of it is almost insurmountable!

In light of the daunting challenge of re-establishing the doctrine of the one-year ministry, it is helpful to look at the origin of the three-year ministry theory. Daniel's prophecy of seventy weeks (9:24–27) is once again prominent:

> Seventy weeks (sevens) are determined upon your people and upon your holy city, to finish the transgression, and to make an end of sins, and to make reconciliation for iniquity, and to bring in everlasting righteousness, and to seal up vision and prophecy, and to anoint the most holy.
>
> Know therefore and understand—from the going forth of the commandment to restore and to build Jerusalem until Messiah the prince shall be seven weeks, and sixty-two weeks. The street shall be built again, and the wall, even in troublesome times.
>
> And after sixty-two weeks Messiah shall be cut-off, but not for Himself: and the people of the prince that shall come shall destroy the city and the sanctuary; and the end thereof shall be with a flood, and to the end of the war desolations are determined.
>
> And he shall confirm the covenant with many for one week: and in the midst of the week he shall cause the sacrifice and the oblation to cease, and for the overspreading of abominations he shall make it desolate, even until the consummation, and that determined shall be poured upon the desolate.

Consider that seventy-weeks were determined and sixty-nine (7+62) were until Messiah's coming. Later the prophecy states that in the middle of the week (assumed by many to be the last of the seventy), Messiah will be cut off (killed).

The teaching of the three-year ministry of Jesus comes from the assumption that seventy weeks are weeks of years (half a week is thus three-and-a-half years), a concept put forward by Eusebius of Caesarea under the patronage of Emperor Constantine the Great (c. 272–c. 337).

Eusebius assumes that the start of the last week in Daniel's prophecy is the start of Jesus' ministry—He ministers for three-and-a-half years and then is killed. There are a multitude of explainations as to how the second half of the week is fulfilled.

As Daniel's prophecy is to the Jews, the gentile Roman Christians of the fourth century say the end of Daniel's prophecy is when God cut off the Jews and turned to the gentiles. However, with the three-year ministry theory, an interpretation of a prophecy is dictating the understanding of Scripture when it should be the other way around! Scripture should dictate the understanding of prophecy.

The three-year ministry theory is flimsy and rests only on this interpretation of Daniel's prophecy. Additional proof affirming a one-year ministry disproves the three-year ministry.

11.2. Manuscript Evidence

Though extant manuscript evidence is the weakest category of support for the one-year ministry, it is important to note that evidence in this category does exist relating to the verse John 6:4, which states:

> And the Passover, a Feast of the Jews, was near.

In New Testament Greek manuscripts (MSS.) 163, 742, 850, 1634, and 2206, John 6:4 is omitted. In MSS. 156, 178, 187, 472, 748, 1177, 2525, and 2684, the verse is marked with an obelus, meaning the scribe who copied it considered the verse spurious, corrupt, or doubtful.

Though most MSS. include John 6:4, the three-year ministry theory has been dominant for the last 1,700 years. This likely led to confirmation bias and those MSS. that included John 6.4 being copied more than those that did not.

Thus, the greater number of MSS. containing John 6:4 may not be a determining factor in deciding which MS. stream stems from the original; other supporting categories of evidence should be considered alongside this one.

11.3. Jesus, the Law-Breaker?

Of interest to Christian readers is that Jesus not attending the added Passover of John 6:4 would make Him a breaker of the Law of Moses; and, as Christians, we believe that Jesus fulfilled the Law on our behalf.

τῇ γ΄ τῆς ε΄ ἑβδ. ἐπάρας ὁ Ἰς τοὺς ὀφθαλμούς·

παρὰ ἀλλήλων λαμβάνοντες. καὶ τὴν

δόξαν τὴν παρὰ τοῦ μόνου

οὐ ζητεῖτε. μὴ δοκεῖτε ὅτι

κατηγορήσω ὑμῶν πρὸς τὸν πατέρα·

ἔστιν ὁ κατηγορῶν ὑμῶν Μωσῆς

εἰς ὃν ὑμεῖς ἠλπίκατε. εἰ γὰρ ἐπι-

στεύετε Μωσεῖ, ἐπιστεύετε ἂν ἐμοί·

περὶ γὰρ ἐμοῦ ἐκεῖνος ἔγραψεν.

εἰ δὲ τοῖς ἐκείνου γράμμασιν οὐ

πιστεύετε, πῶς τοῖς ἐμοῖς ῥήμασι

πιστεύσετε. μετὰ ταῦτα ἀπῆλ-

θεν ὁ Ἰς πέραν τῆς θαλάσσης τῆς

Γαλιλαίας τῆς Τιβεριάδος. καὶ

ἠκολούθει αὐτῷ ὄχλος πολύς, ὅτι

ἑώρων αὐτοῦ τὰ σημεῖα ἃ ἐποί-

ει ἐπὶ τῶν ἀσθενούντων.

ἀνῆλθε δὲ εἰς τὸ ὄρος ὁ Ἰς. καὶ ἐκεῖ

ἐκάθητο μετὰ τῶν μαθητῶν αὐ-

τοῦ. ἀρχή ἐπάρας οὖν ὁ Ἰς

Τοὺς ὀφθαλμούς, καὶ θεασάμενος ὅτι

πολὺς ὄχλος ἔρχεται πρὸς αὐτόν,

λέγει πρὸς τὸν Φίλιππον. πόθεν

ἀγοράσωμεν ἄρτους ἵνα φάγωσιν

οὗτοι. τοῦτο δὲ ἔλεγε, πειράζων

LEFT: An image of MS. 1634, which does not contain John 6:4. Image used with the permission of the Monastery of Megisti Lavra.

It is clear from John 6:4 that Jesus skipped this Passover in Jerusalem (if there was one) and stayed in the Galilee with 5,000 men whom He subsequently fed with the bread and fish.

All Jewish males of age were commanded to attend the three major feasts of Jehovah at Jerusalem (Exodus 23:14–17). Passover was one of these feasts, and if Jesus did not attend it, He would be breaking the Law of Moses.

If Jesus ignored the Law of Moses, it would not make sense for Jesus to say in John 8:46:

> Which of you convicts Me of sin?

There is a clear accusation against Him with regards to this Passover if He skipped it. The Christian reader, therefore, is left with a difficult question! Was Jesus a law-breaker? Or is John 6:4 added to the Bible?

11.4. Early Christian Writers

At best the earliest extant MS. of John 6:4 is from the fourth century. Investigating whether this verse was in earlier copies of the Gospel of John (John) can be done by turning to the writings of the early Christians, deducing its veracity.

The first writer reviewed is Clement of Alexandria (c. 150–c. 215), who wrote in *The Stromata, Book I,* Ch. XXI:

> And Jesus was coming to His baptism, being about thirty years old … And it was necessary for Him to preach only a year, this also is written: "He hath sent Me to proclaim the acceptable year of the Lord." This both the prophet [Isaiah 61:2] spoke, and the Gospel [Luke 4:18–19].

The question arising from this writing is: How could Clement say this if the added Passover of John 6:4 was in his copy of John?

This is also seen in the writings of Origen of Alexandria (c. 185–c. 253), who wrote in his *First Principles, Book IV,* Ch. V:

> [Jesus] taught only during a year and some months.

He also said in *Homilies on Luke* (4:19):

> Following the simple sense of the text, some say that the Saviour preached the Gospel in Judea for only one year, and that this is what the passage "to preach an acceptable year of the Lord" means.

Unfortunately, Origen's commentary on John 6 is damaged. Whether there was a Passover in John 6 can be deduced, however, through Origen's writings on the unnamed Feast in John 5. Consider this entry from *Commentary on John, Book XIII,* Paras. 258–259:

> But we must reply [to those who say the unnamed feast in John 5 is a Passover], that when He came into Galilee [in John 2 just before Passover] … where earlier He had made "the water wine" … And after these things there was a feast of the Jews [John 5] and Jesus went up to Jerusalem, at which time He healed the paralytic …
>
> But if this feast [John 5] were that of Passover (for its name is not added), the sequence of the account is cramped, and this is especially the case since a little later [John 7] it is added that "the Jews" feast of Tabernacles was at hand.

It can be safely inferred from this that Origen didn't have John 6:4 in his text either, as he says that the timeline between John 2 and John 7 is too cramped to include a Passover. He says this of John 5, but it must be equally true of John 6.

Evidence also exists in the writings of an opponent of the one-year-ministry theory. Irenaeus of Lyon (c. 130–c. 202) advocated for a ministry that was over ten years!

The critical element to note regarding Irenaeus' writings is that as he tries to make his case for as many Passovers as possible to bolster his claim, he never mentions a Passover in John 6! This is testimony against interest and very powerful evidence for the absence of John 6:4 in the original text of John. Irenaeus also writes on the feeding of the 5,000 (John 6:1–14) with no mention of a Passover in this text.

Not until the fourth century is a significant duality in the texts of John seen. In this period, we see Eusebius of Caesarea (c. 260–c. 339) with it in his text of John, and Tyconius (c. 379–c. 423) working without it in his text.

Valentinus (c. 100–c. 160), Tertullian (c. 160–c. 240), and Julius Africanus (c. 160–c. 240) also believed the Lord's ministry to have been around one year long.[14]

11.5. Prophecy

As already reviewed, Amos 3:7 reads:

> God does nothing without first revealing it to His servants the prophets.

The above verse being true, we should see some clue of the length of Messiah's ministry in the Old Testament as a prelude.

As discussed, the Eusebian interpretation of Daniel 9, if correct, gives a highly interpretive clue as to the length of Messiah's ministry. This is an incorrect interpretation of Daniel's prophecy, and a clearer clue is given in Isaiah 61:2 of the ministry's length:

> To proclaim the acceptable year of Jehovah (the Lord).

This is a clear statement of the length of ministry, and the parable of the barren fig tree mentioned earlier (section 8.2) is a second witness to this.

Isaiah's prophecy of an acceptable year is strengthened by Jesus' declaration in the Nazareth synagogue (Luke 4:17–21) that He was now fulfilling that prophecy:

> The Spirit of Jehovah is upon Me, because He has anointed Me to proclaim the gospel to the poor; He has sent Me to heal the broken hearted, to proclaim deliverance to the captives, and recovery of sight to the blind, to set at liberty those that are oppressed; and to proclaim the acceptable year of Jehovah (the Lord).

11.5.1. Daniel's Seventy-Week Prophecy

Those who are familiar with Daniel's prophecy will understand that I have not yet explained one of the seventy weeks.

Daniel's prophecy of seventy weeks are two prophecies presented together. This can be seen by a careful reading of the text. The first part of the prophecy reads:

> Seventy weeks (sevens) are determined upon your people and upon your holy city, to finish the transgression, and to make an end of sins, and to make reconciliation for iniquity, and to bring in everlasting righteousness, and to seal up the vision and prophecy, and to anoint the most holy.

Where the prophecy says, "Seventy weeks are determined upon your people and upon your holy city," it is speaking of the Jews (Daniel's people).

The mistake expositors historically have made is assuming the full seventy weeks are part of the calculation of the time of Messiah's coming.

This part of the prophecy shows the length of the ministry, not when it will take place. The seventy weeks are of days (490 days) not years, which will be broken down shortly. Let's first look at the next part of the prophecy (Daniel 9:25–26):

> Know therefore and understand—from the going forth of the commandment to restore and to build Jerusalem until Messiah the prince shall be seven weeks, and sixty-two weeks. The street shall be built again, and the wall, even in troublesome times. And after sixty-two weeks Messiah shall be cut-off.

This is the part of the prophecy that speaks of when Messiah will come. It is after the sixty-two-week period, which itself comes after the seven-week period. Sixty-nine (7 + 62) multiplied by 360 days gives 173,880 days from the decree to restore and rebuild Jerusalem (Nehemiah 2) until Messiah is killed.

The problem created when Daniel's prophecy is read as one is that we end up with Eusebius' confused rendering, or Father Francesco Ribera's (Jesuit Priest c. 1537–c. 1591) interpretation that the seventieth week of Daniel is yet to be fulfilled and will be fulfilled in the future by a seven-year period of the rule of antichrist.

This 2,000-year gap between the sixty-ninth and seventieth week of Daniel is highly interpretive. However, if there are two prophecies, and the seventy weeks refers to the length of Messiah's ministry, then both prophecies have been fulfilled and there is no need of a highly interpretive coming week.

11.5.2. The Seventy-Week Pattern

When considering the length of Jesus' ministry, a pattern is seen in the text of the four Gospels when an acceptable year of Jehovah (the Lord) is assumed:

- Baptism to first Passover (~8 weeks)
- Acceptable year of Jehovah (~54.5 weeks)

- Crucifixion to resurrection (~0.5 weeks)
- Resurrection to Pentecost (7 weeks)

Jesus' baptism to the start of the Passion Week makes sixty-two weeks; then there is one week, in the middle of which Messiah is killed.

The resurrection concludes the Passion Week, and then the seven-week count-down to Pentecost starts as outlined in Leviticus 23. This ends the seventy weeks of Daniel's prophecy with the next day being Pentecost—a new epoch in the history of mankind.

To make this formula work, a thirteen-month Hebrew year is required, this being another proof that the year of the crucifixion is AD 31.

11.5.3. Date of Baptism and Pentecost

With the earlier mentioned dates of Passover in AD 30 and 31, it's now an easy matter to calculate the date of Jesus' baptism and Pentecost using the seventy-week (490 day) framework.

Given that Pentecost is fifty days after Firstfruits, the date of Pentecost is calculated first, then the baptism can be calculated by deducting 490 days from the day before Pentecost.

- Baptism, February 12, AD 30
- Pentecost, June 17, AD 31

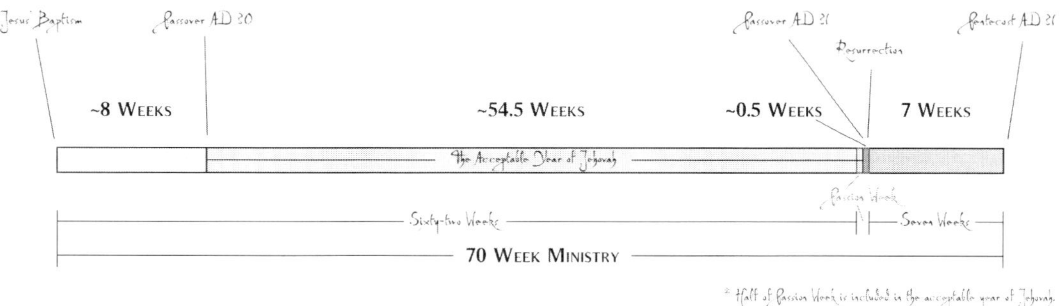

12. Internal Proof of Jesus' One-Year Ministry

In this section I will point to three specific examples of how the one-year ministry makes sense of the text of the Gospels in a way the three-year ministry does not.

The ultimate proof of which theory is correct is in the question: Does the theory improve or confuse the clarity of the Gospel texts?

For the last 1,700 years, the three-year-ministry theory has reigned supreme, and the result has been confusion—a vague understanding of the text with a multitude of seeming contradictions.

The one-year ministry theory, however, adds a clarity and knowability to the Gospels as a historical account of Jesus' ministry that even lay people can understand.

Scripture offers several affirmations, including the order of the Feasts, Jesus' own words, and the chronology of Luke and John.

12.1. Order of Feasts

As discussed earlier, taking out the alleged Passover in John 6:4 reveals that the Feasts presented in the Gospel of John are in perfect order:

- First Passover, April AD 30 (John 2)
- Pentecost, May AD 30 (John 5)
- Tabernacles, September AD 30 (John 7)
- Dedication, December AD 30 (John 10)
- Crucifixion Passover, April AD 31 (John 13)

Of course, the feast in John 5 is unnamed, but the timeline in John makes it clear that it is Pentecost.

12.2. My Time Has Not Yet Come

Under the three-year ministry paradigm, Jesus' words to His mother in John 2:4, "My time has not yet come," are confusing and appear as if He needed a push from Mary to get His ministry started.

Under the one-year ministry theory, however, it becomes clear that the wedding feast in Cana, where He says this, happened around a week before the first Passover of Jesus' ministry.

All of Jesus' public miracles happen between the first and second Passover, which is within a one-year period. Jesus saying His time had not yet come clearly refers to this "acceptable year of Jehovah" as outlined by Isaiah, making sense of this saying of Jesus.

12.3. Chronology of Luke and John

One interesting aspect of the one-year ministry is that it takes seriously the apparent chronology of Luke and John. These two Gospels can be spliced together under the one-year framework and give a consistent and logical account of Jesus' ministry.

The Gospel of Mark, too, is very consistent with Luke and John, although it does vary the chronology of some inter-week events—however, over the broader time frame, it is consistent.

The Gospel of Matthew is the outlier, showing little chronological consistency with the other three. It should be noted, however, it is difficult to see anyone making a case for a chronology in Matthew that is plausible under any timeframe of Jesus' ministry.

It seems apparent that Matthew was the first Gospel written and was grouped into sections rather than ever being intended to be a chronological account of Jesus' ministry. A hint of this can be seen in this comment by Papias of Hierapolis (c. 60–c. 130) quoted in Eusebius' *Church History, Book III,* Ch. XXXIX:

> Therefore Matthew put the *logia* in an ordered arrangement in the Hebrew language, but each person interpreted them as best he could.

Papias thought Matthew was chronological in comparison to Mark; however, given the weight of evidence of the consistency of Mark, Luke, and John, this seems untenable.

Importantly, Papias' quote is strong evidence that Matthew was first written in Hebrew, and it seems the multiple Greek translations of it were suboptimal. It may be that the Hebrew Gospel of Matthew was never intended to be chronological and that the interpreter(s) may have added the few chronological joining words between events to make it seem so.

My opinion on Matthew is of course speculative, but, given the weight of three Gospels versus one, I think the chronology of Luke and John, in particular, should be viewed as superior—especially so when other supporting evidence for the one-year ministry is strong.

13. Summary

A theory being historically true should have several diverse proofs as to its accuracy. Each category of proof should also be consistent with other categories.

Consider now the degree of confidence in these findings best done by revisiting the earlier graphic:

	AD 27	AD 28	AD 29	AD 30	AD 31	AD 32	AD 33	AD 34
30th of John & 3+1					Y	Y		
Day of Week		Y			Y			Y
Blood Moon					Y		Y	
13th Month		Y	Y		Y			Y
69-Weeks Prophecy					Y	Y		
Strength of Argument		**40%**	**20%**		**100%**	**40%**	**20%**	**20%***

A high degree of confidence should be attached to AD 31 not just because it is the strongest candidate in the field but because it is consistent with every category of evidence that is credible to use when trying to triangulate the date of Messiah's crucifixion.

While some will argue against some of the explanations in this paper, there is another powerful way to visualise the case for AD 31. The following graphic shows the years ruled out because they did not meet one of the two inarguable criteria:

	AD 27	AD 28	AD 29	AD 30	AD 31	AD 32	AD 33	AD 34
Day of Week	X		X	X		X	X	
Blood Moon	X	X	X	X		X		X

Only AD 31 doesn't fail at least one of these two critical categories.

There will be those who still say that even these two categories are disputable, but if the text is not taken seriously, then nothing is knowable—everything is speculation and interpretation. When studied diligently, it is clear from the text that both a Wednesday crucifixion and a blood moon on Passover are needed.

The fact that this result can be produced speaks to the veracity of the text and that these dates have been preserved both in the text and in the ancient biblical Hebrew calendar system.

13.1. Why Now after 2,000 Years?

It is fair to ask why these dates have now been found when a multitude of intelligent scholars over the last 2,000 years have not been able to find them. No lesser genius than Sir Isaac Newton has applied himself to this task and was unable to come up with anything convincing.

The answer isn't in the intelligence of the men who have studied this issue but rather in the resurgence of the biblical Hebrew calendar these dates are preserved in.

As previously stated, the biblical calendar system is a lunar system corrected to the sun periodically by the agricultural season. A few people have been working over the last few decades to understand and teach the biblical calendar system, the most prominent of whom are Michael Rood and Nehemiah Gordon.

Western scholars have been working under the handicap of seeing things through the Western solar calendar system (pagan in origin), the three-year ministry theory, and a Friday crucifixion.

These false paradigms have held back our understanding and placed, as it were, a veil over our eyes.

13.2. This Situation Foretold

> He shall speak pompous words against the Most High, shall persecute the saints of the Most High, and shall intend to change times and law.

This quote is from Daniel 7:25 (sixth century BC), and the "he" is generally taken by Christians to be antichrist.

I will not look at the changing of law in this summary; however, the changing of times is relevant to this paper as it explains why the dates and times of Messiah have been hidden from us.

With the apparent Christianisation of Rome in the fourth century, the following took place:

- The council of Nicaea decided to separate Easter from the biblical date of the Jewish Passover; and
- The Romans declared Christmas was to be celebrated on December 25, coinciding with the popular pagan celebration of Saturnalia.

According to Professor Mark Del Cogliano in *Reconsidering Eusebius,* p. 44:

> It was not the Quartodeciman [14th of Nisan] practice that Constantine sought to eliminate but rather the so-called "Protopaschite" practice, which calculated the paschal [Passover] full moon according to the Jewish lunar calendar and not the Julian solar calendar.

Christian Rome's break with the Jewish Feasts given by God and merger with the existing paganism of the empire lead to a loss of biblical Hebrew context, which ensured the understanding of the dates and times of Messiah were locked away under a foreign paradigm.

To prove my point, consider the words of emperor Constantine—a leading player in establishing a Christianity disconnected from its Jewish roots. Eusebius in his book *Life of Constantine* quotes him as saying:

> It appeared an unworthy thing that in the celebration of this most holy feast [Passover] we should follow the practice of the Jews, who have impiously defiled their hands with enormous sin [killing Christ] … Let us then have nothing in common with the detestable Jewish crowd; for we have received from our Saviour a different way.

What is seen at the council of Nicaea, in a way, is the official divorce of gentile Christianity from its Jewish roots and the establishment of the Roman Catholic Church proper.

13.3. Summary of Dates

For the first time since the first century, the full set of dates of Messiah's ministry are known (Hebrew and Julian dates shown):

- Birth of John the Baptist, Passover 3 BC (March 31)
- Birth of Jesus, Tabernacles 3 BC (September 26)
- Magi visit infant Jesus, Kislev 23, 2 BC (December 21)
- John the Baptist begins his ministry, Passover AD 27 (April 11)
- Jesus baptised by John, February 12, AD 30
- Beginning of the acceptable year of Jehovah, Passover AD 30 (April 7)
- Jesus crucified, Passover AD 31 (April 25)
- The resurrection, Firstfruits AD 31 (April 28)
- The ascension, June 7, AD 31
- Giving of the Holy Spirit, Pentecost AD 31 (June 17)

13.4. Implications

That a written text claiming to be from God and astronomical observations come together—as outlined in this paper—proves beyond a reasonable doubt that the same guiding hand was behind the creation of both.

Prophecies provably written hundreds of years before the corresponding events take place are one of the strongest types of evidence for a supernatural being beyond space and time.

Apart from being the best candidate for Messiah, Jesus came at the time foretold by the prophet Daniel—an absolute proof of His claim to being the Messiah, as the distant second-best candidate in this timeframe is John the Baptist, and he clearly stated that he was *not* the Messiah, pointing to the one coming directly after him (Matthew 3:11).

The fact that "Christianity" has been operating under the three-year ministry model for 1,700 years is a proof that what is called Christianity today has some foundational errors in it.

The dominance of the three-year ministry doctrine also shows how powerful tradition is within the church and that pure Christianity should be taken only from Scripture—as tradition often contradicts the plain reading of the text.

13.5. Further Reading

My book *The Gospel of Messiah* has used the theories presented in this paper to combine the four Gospels into one chronological account of the life and ministry of Jesus Christ. How this book reads is one of the greatest tests and proofs of the theory's correctness. A free online copy is available at the website www.gospelofmessiah.com for those wishing to study this subject matter further.

The website may also be accessed by following this QR code:

Endnotes

1 The explanation that requires the fewest assumptions is usually correct.

2 Northern Hemisphere.

3 https://en.wikipedia.org/wiki/Abrahamic_religions

4 Some try to use the building of the temple by Herod to date Jesus' ministry, assuming Herod began to build the temple in the eighteenth year of his reign. Josephus tells us Herod undertook to build the temple during this year; however, there may have been a few years of planning before actual building commenced. I have found this dating method to be unreliable when compared to the methods I have used in this paper.

5 Image generated in Starry Night, by Simulation Curriculum.

6 I am using the term Passover loosely when referring to John's birthday. The Passover lamb was killed on Nisan 14 and eaten that night, being Nisan 15 (days change at sunset). John was likely born on the day of the Passover meal (Nisan 15), not on the day the Passover lamb was killed (Nisan 14).

7 *The Chronological Gospels*, pp. 37–39.

8 *The Chronological Gospels*, pp. 51–56.

9 *The Chronological Gospels*, pp. 57–61.

10 There is a possibility that AD 34 also had a Wednesday Passover; however, it is unlikely.

11 https://eclipse.gsfc.nasa.gov/5MCLE/5MCLE-Figs-05.pdf

12 https://en.wikipedia.org/wiki/Artaxerxes_I

13 Anderson, *The Coming Prince*, 10th Edition, Ch. 6, p. 78

14 Much of what has been discussed in this section comes from the work of Nehemiah Gordon: https://youtu.be/Y9U0v-TFPFY?si=LijNfrpPuvuLy6Rh

Appendices

A. Matthew's Account

The Gospel of Matthew (26:17) says:

> Now on the first *day of the Feast* of Unleavened Bread the disciples came to Jesus, saying to Him, "Where do You wish us to prepare for You to eat the Passover?"

Notice the italics in the text. These words are not there in the Greek, rather are interposed by the English translators. Thus, it more correctly reads: "on the first of Unleavened Bread."

This is ambiguous, leaving open the possibility that Matthew was writing about an earlier day of preparation for the Feast. Also note that the first day of the Feast of Unleavened Bread is Nisan 15 and Passover is Nisan 14. Thus, if we take the text as translated in English literally, Passover is already past, and there is a contradiction.

Later in Matthew 27:62 we see the following event the day after Jesus was crucified:

> On the next day, which followed the Day of Preparation, the chief priests and Pharisees gathered together to Pilate, saying, "Sir, we remember that deceiver said, while He was yet alive, 'After three days I will rise.'"

Preparation Day is the day the Passover lamb was killed (Nisan 14), meaning, by this text, Jesus was killed on Passover, as I am asserting. How, then, can Jesus have eaten the Passover the night before He was executed if He was executed on Passover?

The proponents of a Thursday night Passover and Good Friday crucifixion not only make Matthew contradict John but also make Matthew contradict himself.

B. Mark's Account

In Mark's Gospel account (14:12), he says:

> Now on the first day of Unleavened Bread, when they killed the Passover, His disciples said to Him, "Where do You wish us to go and prepare, that You may eat the Passover?"

Technically the first day of Unleavened Bread is Nisan 15; however, Mark seems to be using the term loosely here. Notice, though, what Mark 15:42–43 says, just after Jesus had been crucified:

> Now when evening had come, because it was the Preparation Day, that is, the day before the Sabbath, Joseph of Arimathea, an honourable member of the council, who was himself waiting for the kingdom of God, came, and taking courage, went into Pilate and asked for the body of Jesus.

This text in Mark clearly shows that Jesus was killed on Preparation Day (Nisan 14), which contradicts Mark 14:12 if this part of the account is taken as Passover. It should also be noted that the nighttime part of Nisan 14 comes before the daytime part of Nisan 14 when the Passover lambs were slaughtered. Thus, the Last Supper by my reckoning was technically on Passover Nisan 14; however, it was not the Passover meal itself as this was eaten on Nisan 15 after sunset.

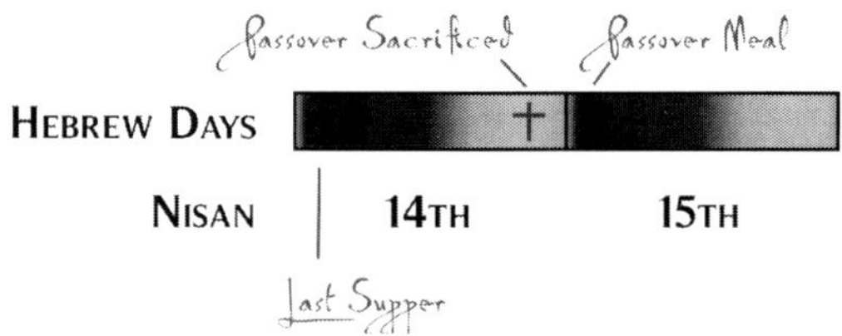

Potential Objection: Some will claim that the Preparation Day was the day of preparation before the weekly Sabbath. While they can cite some extrabiblical sources as support, it should be noted that only the day when the Passover was killed was clearly called Preparation Day in the Bible.

C. Luke's Account

In Luke 22:15–18 we see Jesus eating the Last Supper with His disciples:

> Then He said to them, "With desire I have desired to eat this Passover with you before I suffer; for I say to you, I will no longer eat of it until it is fulfilled in the kingdom of God." Then He took the cup, and gave thanks, and said, "Take this and divide it among yourselves; for I say to you, I will not drink of the fruit of the vine until the kingdom of God comes."

Some will use this passage as clear evidence the Last Supper was the Passover meal, and if taken on its own, would be the most likely conclusion. However, all the scriptural evidence must be weighed together. In light of other evidence, this passage could be taken to mean that Jesus desired to eat the coming Passover with them but would not until it was fulfilled in the kingdom of God. There is no evidence of a lamb being eaten at this meal as the Passover ordinance required.

Note also that in Luke 23:54, Jesus was clearly crucified on the Preparation Day (the Passover sacrifice), so He could not have eaten the Passover meal itself. Again, we see a synoptic Gospel contradicting itself if the Last Supper is taken as the Passover meal.

D. John's Account

While a Last Supper Passover can be argued somewhat from the synoptic Gospels, John is unmistakable that Jesus was killed on Passover. This is seen in the following chronology of events in the Gospel of John:

- 13:1–2 Last Supper being eaten before the Feast of Passover.
- 13:29 Disciples think Jesus tells Judas to buy those things needed for the Feast at the Last Supper.
- 18:28 Jewish leaders won't enter the gentile judgment hall with Jesus because they do not want to defile themselves that they may eat the Passover.
- 19:14 Pilate brings Jesus to the judgment seat on preparation for Passover.
- 19:31 Jews ask for the bodies to be taken off the crosses, for the approaching day was a high day (Nisan 15).
- 19:42 Disciples laid Jesus in the tomb because it was Preparation Day (Nisan 14).

E. The Gospels Combined

When deciding when the Passover fell in the Gospels, we have two clear choices:

1. Massage the wording in Matthew, Mark, and Luke a little to fit with the Gospel of John and also make the three synoptic Gospels internally consistent with themselves; or,
2. Massage the wording in Matthew, Mark, and Luke to make them internally consistent with themselves and then tear the crucifixion account in the Gospel of John out of the Bible!

It is easy to conceive that early gentile Christian scribes misunderstood the timing of the Passover and used a couple of different Greek words regarding the timing of the

Feast that have confused the chronology somewhat, but it is another thing to say that one of the four Gospels has a fundamental error.

To make my point, look at the minimal changes that need to be made to bring the four Gospels into line and clear up the inconsistencies in the synoptics:

- Matthew 26:17 — Understand this text as *before* Unleavened Bread and not *the first day* of Unleavened Bread.
- Matthew 26:17 — Understand the disciples' Passover preparation was not necessarily for that night's dinner.
- Mark 14:12 — Understand that Passover preparations can take more than one day.
- Luke 22:7 — Understand *Then came the day* as *Then approached the day* of Unleavened Bread.

That's it! Those are the only changes needed to make all of the Gospels consistent with themselves and each other, not to mention lining up with Paul's statement that Jesus was our Passover, sacrificed for us (1 Corinthians 5:7).

Compare this to the literary violence of saying the three synoptic Gospels are inconsistent and the Gospel of John is flat-out wrong, and the choice becomes clear.

Those who say Jesus wasn't sacrificed on Passover have missed the prophetic significance of the Old Testament and how accurately it foretells Christ's coming and ministry.

F. Conceding Some Ground

Scholars have put forward dates for the Passover for each of the candidate years of Jesus' crucifixion. Also, despite the evidence I have presented, many will still insist on a Friday crucifixion. Given this, I thought it helpful to construct a table showing the years with both a possible Wednesday and Friday crucifixion.

Also, where it was arguable which full moon of the year the Passover would fall, which day it would fall, or if it was a thirteen-month year—I have conceded all possibilities.

With these factors conceded, the Strength of Argument table now looks like this:

	AD 27	AD 28	AD 29	AD 30	AD 31	AD 32	AD 33	AD 34
30th of John & 3+1					Y	Y		
Day of Week	Y	Y		Y	Y		Y	Y
Blood Moon					Y		Y	
13th Month		Y	Y		Y			Y
69-Weeks Prophecy					Y	Y		
Strength of Argument	**20%**	**40%**	**20%**	**20%**	**100%**	**40%**	**40%**	**20%***

* *The year AD 34 may have either a Wednesday Passover or thirteen-month year but cannot have both. Hence, I have only counted one of the Yeses in the Strength of Argument calculation.*

G. The Temple Reference

Some will notice that I did not use the Jew's reference to the building of the temple in John 2:20 to triangulate my date of AD 31:

> Then the Jews said, "Forty-six years was this temple in building, and will You raise it up in three days?"

It is clear from Josephus' *Antiquities of the Jews, Book XV,* Para. 380 that King Herod the Great purposed to rebuild the temple in Jerusalem in a larger form than existed at that time. Most will agree that this was in the year 20 BC.

What is unclear is how long it took King Herod to begin building the temple. Josephus in *Antiquities, Book XV,* Para. 388 relates that the Jews were concerned that Herod would pull down the old edifice and then be unable to complete the rebuild, given the scope of the project. In light of this, Herod promises the Jews that he will not begin the demolition until everything is ready for the new temple (Para. 389).

Josephus then relates (Para. 390) that these preparations included the procurement of 1,000 wagons to carry the materials, the selection of 10,000 skilled workmen, and the training of some of the priests in stone cutting and carpentry.

While Josephus doesn't state it, I think these preparatory works would have included the quarrying and sourcing of enough materials to at least begin the build and reassure the Jews that the project could and would be completed.

The foundational questions are then: How long did these preparatory works take? And also: Was the preparation for the rebuilding of the temple included in the comment in John 2:20 that the temple had been forty-six years in building at the time of that Passover?

Counting forward forty-six years from 20 BC comes out at 27 AD (remember, no year zero). However, if three years of preparations are factored in before the build begins, it comes out at my year of 30 AD for the first Passover of Jesus' ministry. I have left this factor out of my theory as I think this line of evidence is debatable, and it is unclear which date it supports, if any.

MESSIAH
MATTHEW, MARK
LUKE AND JOHN
BRETT HOOPER

Made in United States
Cleveland, OH
14 August 2025

19391541R00030